ARTISAN
ROPEWORK

ARTISAN
ROPEWORK

15 3-D Stitched
Rope Craft projects

JESSICA GEACH

SCHIFFER
PUBLISHING

4880 Lower Valley Road · Atglen, PA 19310

© 2022 Design and layout by BlueRed Press
© 2022 Text and step images by Jessica Geach

Photo credits

All photos by the author except:
The Really Good Media Company—cover, pp. 2, 4, 6, 8, 26, 28, 33, 34, 38, 42, 47, 48, 53, 54, 58, 60, 64, 69, 70, 76, 80, 86, 88, 94, 99, 100, 107, 108, 115, 116(BR), 122(B).
Viola Depic—p. 127.

Library of Congress Control Number: 2021944646

Produced by BlueRed Press Ltd. 2022
Designed by Eleanor Forty-Robbins
Type set in Montserrat

ISBN: 978-0-7643-6306-1
Printed in India

Published by Schiffer Publishing, Ltd.
4880 Lower Valley Road
Atglen, PA 19310
Phone: (610) 593-1777; Fax: (610) 593-2002
Email: Info@schifferbooks.com
Web: www.schifferbooks.com

For our complete selection of fine books on this and related subjects, please visit our website at www.schifferbooks.com. You may also write for a free catalog.

Schiffer Publishing's titles are available at special discounts for bulk purchases for sales promotions or premiums. Special editions, including personalized covers, corporate imprints, and excerpts, can be created in large quantities for special needs. For more information, contact the publisher.

We are always looking for people to write books on new and related subjects. If you have an idea for a book, please contact us at proposals@schifferbooks.com.

Other Schiffer Books on Related Subjects:
The Art of Contemporary Woven Paper Basketry, Dorothy McGuiness, ISBN 978-0-7643-6213-2
Basketry Basics, BJ Crawford, ISBN 978-0-7643-5745-9
Andean Sling Braids, Roderick Owen & Terry Newhouse Flynn, ISBN 978-0-7643-5103-7

Contents

Introduction

Artisan ropework is a satisfying and addictive handicraft that can be used to make an amazing range of fantastic 3-D things. I have a lifelong passion for textiles and tactile objects, and while exploring this as an artist, I quickly discovered that unbleached cotton rope is my absolute favorite material to work with! The way it is braided makes it so soft and fantastically strong, all while remaining wonderfully flexible.

I am endlessly fascinated by the process of turning piles of rope into tactile, purposeful bags, baskets, and homewares. My passion for exploring textiles inspired me to found my own textile studio—Ruby Cubes—in 2015, and I have been working there full time ever since, exploring tactile and purposeful 3-D objects made from rope.

I am greatly inspired by the amazing diversity of the landscape that surrounds me. I am lucky enough to live on Dartmoor, in the far southwest of England, which means that I am never far from breathtaking hilltops, refreshing river walks, or the stunning Devonshire coastline. My explorations in shape and color are often informed by rambles through the wild.

I have spent a number of years deeply exploring the endless possibilities that artisan ropework has to offer, and in this book I'm going to share with you the secrets to mastering this immensely satisfying craft.

Once you have conquered the basics, you'll be amazed at how quickly your sewing table will be full of beautiful and purposeful objects that you can gift or use around your own home.

Tools, Materials, and Techniques

To get started on your artisan ropework journey, you will need a few basic tools to help you on your way. I am sure that you will already own some of these things in your existing sewing kits, but it can be helpful to gather what you need in one place before starting so that you can easily access the tool you need when you need it.

Tools and Materials

The three most important elements in stitched ropework are

· the rope

· the sewing machine

· the thread

Over the next few pages you'll find a comprehensive explanation about all these elements to help you get started. I've also listed other useful tools at the end, and these are referred to as your "general sewing kit" in the materials list for each project.

Rope supplies can be purchased from good craft stores, online, and from *www.rubycubes.co.uk*.

Rope

To make 3-D objects that are strong in structure, it is important to use the right type of rope. It needs to be fully braided—which means it is not hollow like a piping cord. I work with an unbleached, braided cotton rope in 3 mm, 6 mm, or 8 mm widths. Rope and thread properties are almost always described in metric, since the thinner sizes are most easily described this way. Other measurements in this book are given in both standard and metric forms.

3 mm = 0.12 in.
6 mm = 0.236 in.
8 mm = 0.314 in.

All the projects in this book have been designed and photographed using this unbleached cotton rope. You could, alternatively, use any natural material such as jute, hemp, or flax rope (as long as it is a structural braid and not hollow), each of which will give a different aesthetic to the projects in this book.

Colorful macramé cords and twines, while not being suitable for the main body of stitching, are also a great way to add pops of color to your projects by creating tassels and knots to attach to your stitched shapes. This is an easy and fun way to inject some of your own personality into the projects.

Sewing Machines

All the projects in this book have been made on a domestic sewing machine, specifically my Janome 525S Sewist. When I first started out, I worked with a Janome J3-24, but you should be able to make all the projects described in this book on a standard domestic machine as long as it has a decent zigzag stitch. The more options the machine has for width, the better. As long as it catches both sides of the rope, you'll be set.

You need to use denim or heavyweight needles for all of my projects. Sewing at a steady pace will also be kinder to your machine and give you time to really feel the angle of your work, which is important. You will find, though, that the arm of your sewing machine will greatly dictate how you can explore shape and size within this craft.

Sewing with rope is not like sewing a flat cotton fabric—it is more demanding on the machine, and the lint builds up much more quickly because the needle punches through the rope and releases fiber with every stitch. Clean the lint out regularly and learn to work within the limitations of your machine, and you'll be able to create so many beautiful things. Feel free, however, to alter some of the angles in the projects if your machine is shaped differently from mine.

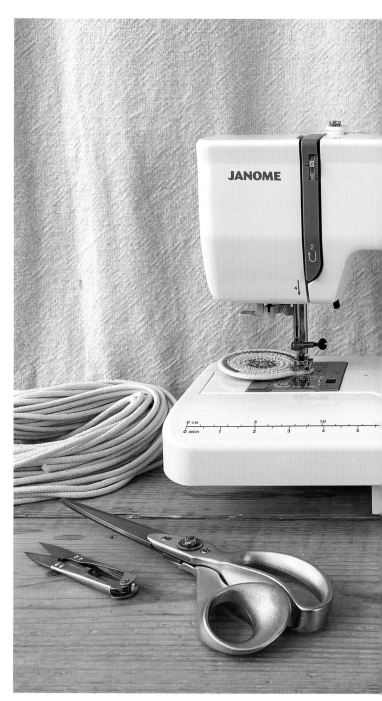

Thread

Whether you choose a natural organic cotton thread or a polyester sew-all version, just make sure it's a high-quality thread. The thread needs to work in harmony with the rope to create tension and build your desired shapes. A good thread will feel strong as you build your shapes. A cheap one will snap or snag easily and be frustrating, rather than satisfying, to work with.

You will also go through significantly more thread than you expect. Zigzag stitching work *eats* thread, so if you have the option, go for 1,000 m spools instead of 100 m, since you will have to change your spool a lot less and you won't run the risk of running out midproject.

Be sure to use the same type of thread for your top and bobbin thread. Also, even if they are different colors, use the same manufacturer. This goes a long way to prevent issues with tension, plus it gives a nicer finish to your work.

A Note about Thread Colors

You will notice that on many of the projects, I have listed in the materials section "neutral thread." This is because unbleached rope is not white. The neutral refers to a shade that is as close as possible to the rope that you are working with. With the unbleached rope you may find an off-white linen is best, or if you are working with jute you may find a fawn-brown color matches well. A trip to your local yarn and thread or craft store with a sample of the rope you want to use may be the best way to achieve the closest thread match.

General Sewing Kit

Ruler: This is essential since you will need to measure your rope lengths and your spiral rounds for each project in the book. A metal ruler is preferable since it will sit nice and flat on the rope, but a plastic one will be just fine if that's what you have.

Sharp fabric scissors: You need to use a really good, sharp pair of scissors to create clean cuts in the rope. Blunt scissors will leave jagged ends, which will be hard to work with. A clean cut will leave a neater finish and be much easier to stitch down.

Snips: Technically not essential, but very useful for trimming threads away since they are easier to maneuver than big scissors when trying to snip away threads. I have multiple pairs in my studio, since I can't do without mine.

Pins: You will need these for marking out sections of rope, as well as gap sections and handles in many of the projects. Invest in a new set of nice sharp pins with colorful heads, since these will sit nicely in the rope and be easy to see. Blunt pins will snag and make it difficult to remove them.

Tassel brush: This is an optional tool, but it can be a great time-saver when making tassel elements for your artisan ropework pieces. The one I use is actually a metal cat hair brush that I bought specifically for working with rope. Be sure to protect your work surface if you use one of these brushes, since the prongs will leave scratches behind. Alternatively, you can use a straight pin or tapestry needle to separate the fibres for smaller tassels.

Project Materials

Cotton twill tape: For the beach bag project, you will need this to make the straps. Try to go for a heavyweight version, which will be sturdier and not twist as easily.

Clay: For the wall-hanging project. Any good-quality, air-drying clay that you can find in hobby shops will give good results.

Textile paint: The wall-hanging project in this book uses paint instead of thread to add color. Paint is a lovely variation instead of colored thread to create a different aesthetic. Any heat-setting textile paint will work with the rope. It is easiest to steam the paint once dry to set it, rather than trying to get the flat of the iron in between all the furrows of the rope.

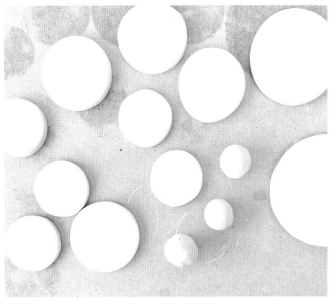

Getting Started

Before you dive into the projects, there's a simple secret to stitching rope that you need to know first.

Essentially, everything in this book is a spiral!

Stitching the rope to itself creates the spiral, and this is the basis for all the shapes you'll find in these projects. So the first thing to understand is how to start your spiral, because this is the key to starting all your projects.

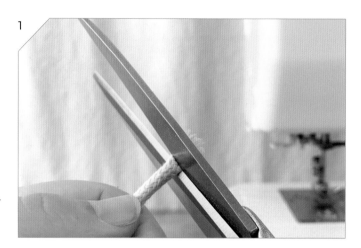

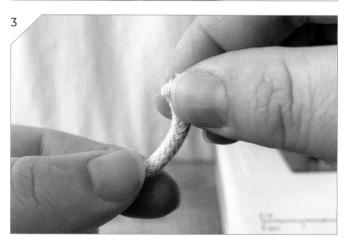

Making a Spiral

Make a nice clean cut on the end of your rope **(1–2)**. Hold the rope with your fingers **(3)**. Use your left hand to pull the rope down at the same time as pulling against it with your right hand **(4)**. Each time, you are allowing the piece in your left hand to gather and start making a spiral **(5)**. Go around a couple more times so there's enough to comfortably hold between your thumb and forefinger **(6)**.

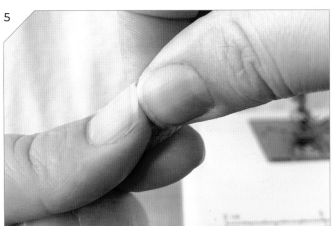

The spiral needs to have sufficient tension to make it feel sturdy, but not so much that your knuckles are blanching holding it **(7)**. If it's too loose, it will fall apart before you can get it under the machine. This might seem basic, but getting the technique right will ensure that all your projects start on a really good foundation.

Slide your spiral into your sewing machine, with the actual spiral on the left and the loose rope to the right **(8)**. Sew backward and forward to secure the stitch and then move the spiral around while at the same time sewing to catch all the sides **(9–11)**. The more stitching you do here, the stronger your spiral will be. This bit of spiral will be the visible middle of your projects, so it's worth taking the time to make it neat and strong.

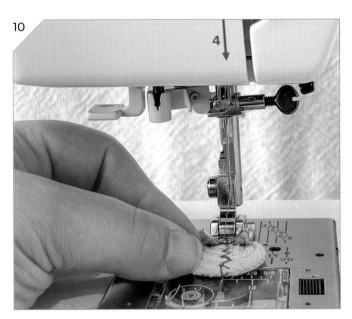

Once you are happy that the middle of your spiral is ready, maneuver it while stitching to the point where the spiral and the loose rope are not yet connected, and trim away the starting threads to prevent these from getting caught up in your sewing machine (12 –14).

Now you are ready to grow the flat spiral.

Hold the loose rope in your right hand and guide the spiral with your left (15). The left hand does all the shaping work in artisan ropework. The right hand keeps tension in the loose rope, while allowing it to flow through the machine at the point where the needle connects the spiral to the rope with the zigzag stitch. With every stitch you make, your spiral grows.

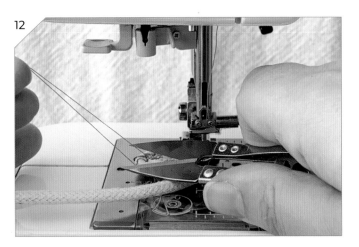

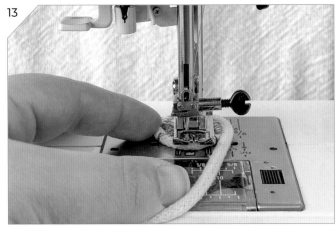

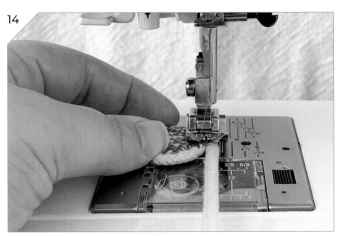

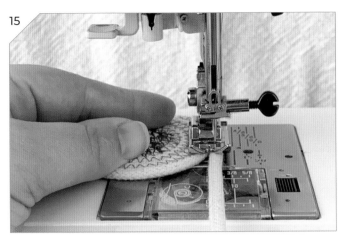

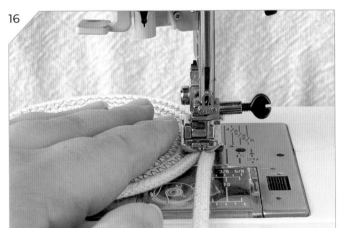

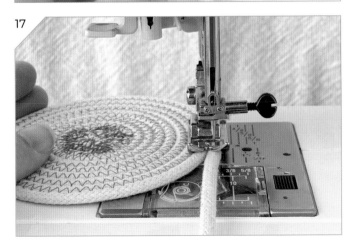

To make a flat spiral, your left hand should keep the angle where the spiral meets the rope completely flat as you stitch (**16–17**). The width of your spiral entirely depends on the project you are working on.

You will see at the beginning of every project that the first step is to "create your starting spiral." For example, the beach bag project requires a starting spiral of 11 in. (28 cm). This means you need to make a flat spiral that is 11 in. wide before building the shape.

Building Shape

Now that you know how to make a flat starting spiral, the next step is to make it 3-D. This is referred to as "building shape." Each project requires a different angle to create the various shapes. Before we get into specifics, let's talk about how you turn a flat spiral into a 3-D spiral.

At the point where you want to turn your flat spiral into a 3-D one, you will need to reposition your left hand. Instead of your left hand being flat on top of the spiral, lift your hand and position it *underneath* the spiral **(18)**. Now you can lift the spiral gently to create an angle. As you stitch, this will turn your flat spiral into a 3-D one.

Lifting the spiral changes the point at which the loose rope connects to it. This is what creates the angle. The steeper you pull the spiral up, the sharper the angle you create **(19)**. As your 3-D spiral grows, you'll find you may need to allow your left hand to move to support the spiral in different places to keep it steady on the machine. Especially with the larger projects, you'll find your hand will end up supporting the piece from the bottom of the spiral.

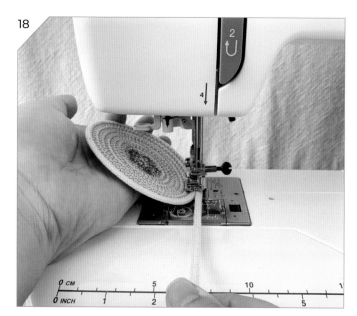

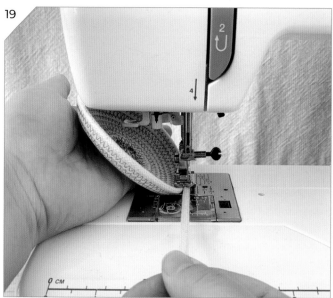

At all times, use your left hand to shape the spiral and your right hand to keep the loose rope flowing through the machine (20–22).

It's inevitable at some point that you will wobble off and there'll be a gap in your spiral (in the more advanced projects, this will be a deliberate technique rather than an accidental one), but don't worry. Stop the machine as soon as you realize—you'll feel the gap before you see it, since the machine won't punch through the rope. Unpick to the point where the spiral gapes, and then start again.

Use a block stitch to resecure the thread—this means doing a forward and reverse stitch over the same small area a number of times to make sure the thread doesn't unravel. Block stitch is used a lot throughout this book as both a structural and a decorative element.

With the technical knowledge of how to make a starting spiral and how to build shape, you are now ready to dive into the projects.

Beginner Projects

This book is written so that, with every project you complete, your skill level in artisan ropework will increase. These first few projects teach you the absolute fundamentals in spiral work and provide you with the foundation you need to achieve great results in the more advanced projects later in the book. Make sure you have read the "Getting Started" chapter, since this goes into the most detail about how to start your spirals and explains the process for building shape.

During the first few projects, concentrate your efforts on making neat spirals and really learning the basic techniques. Block stitch features in every project, so get comfortable with your reverse-stitch lever and allow yourself to engage with how the rope feels in your hands as you begin to build simple shapes. Remember that artisan ropework is a journey among you, the rope, and your sewing machine.

Mats and Coasters

Let's put your knowledge from the "Getting Started" chapter into practice by making a set of four rope mats and coasters. This will give you all the practice you need in making flat spirals, before moving on to the 3-D shapes.

Materials

23 ft. (7 m) × 8 mm,
    unbleached cotton rope (per mat)
5 ft. (1.5 m) × 8 mm,
    unbleached cotton rope (per coaster)
2 contrasting thread colors—
    e.g., red and gold
General sewing kit

Techniques

Block stitch
Loop finish

Mats and Coasters

Method

Start by measuring out all your lengths. You will need four lengths of 23 ft. (7 m) and four of 4.9 ft. (1.5 m). Put your lengths in separate piles so you can easily reach the one you need. To reduce the number of times you need to change thread, you will be working on the mats simultaneously.

Start with a 23 ft. (7 m) length and gold thread and stitch a starting spiral of 3.9 in. (10 cm) **(1)**. Remember to make the middle of your spiral really secure with lots of thread and use your left hand to keep the shape flat. When you reach 10 cm, finish with a little section of block stitching and take the spiral off the machine.

Repeat with your second length of 23 ft. (7 m) and put both spirals to one side. Take a 4.9 ft. (1.5 m) length and stitch a gold spiral to 1.9 in. (5 cm). Finish with block stitching and take off the machine. Repeat with a second length of 4.9 ft. (1.5 m).

You now have two mats and two coasters in progress. Switch to the red thread and repeat this process with the remaining 23 ft. (7 m) and 4.9 ft. (1.5 m) lengths. Now all your mats and coasters are in progress.

Remaining with your red thread, take the gold spirals you started. Secure the thread with a section of block stitching and continue to stitch flat until you have 5.9 in. (15 cm) of rope left at the end **(2–6)**. Be mindful that the point at which the spiral connects with the loose rope at the needlepoint is where any shaping happens—so make sure your left hand keeps the angle completely flat where the two ropes meet.

With the last section of rope, let's use a loop technique to finish your mat. Loops are a wonderful way to finish rope projects, because it means that they can be stored on hooks when not in use.

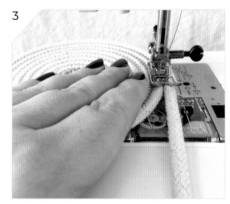

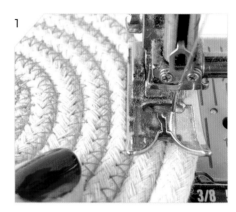

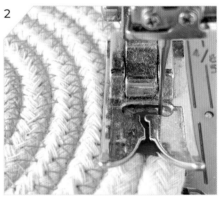

4

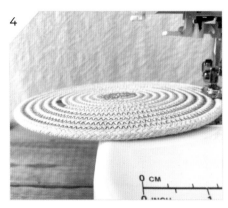

5

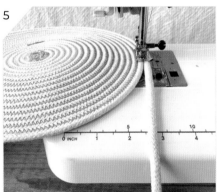

6

7

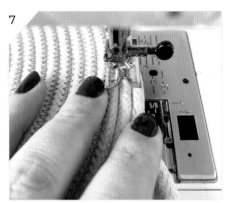

8

9

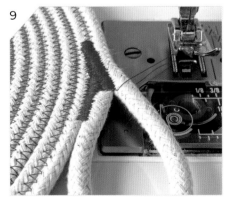

Loop Finish Technique

To make a loop, keep your needle in the left side of the work (in the spiral) and lift the presser foot (7–9). Cut the end of the rope with sharp scissors so you are working with a clean edge. Push the end of the rope back into the section next to where the needle is: pinch it all together to keep it in place, and put the presser foot down.

Now you have two sections that need to be firmly stitched to make the loop secure—the section between the spiral and the end, and the end with the loose rope on the right. Block-stitch over the whole area until it is thoroughly secure.

10

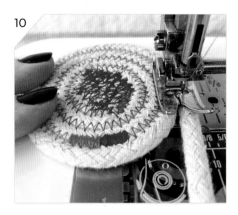

11

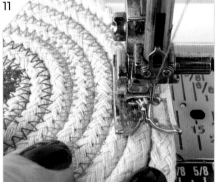

12

13

14

When the first mat is complete, go through the others in turn and finish them in red or gold thread, all with a loop finish so they match **(10–14)**. Use exactly the same loop technique each time to finish the coasters.

Your new rope mats and coasters will level up your dining-table game. And now that you are proficient in making flat spirals, you are ready for the 3-D projects ahead.

Key Rings

This is a fun little project that's a great way to use up the small offcuts that quickly accumulate from other projects. Try experimenting with lots of different colors, since it's an easy way to see how different shades look on your rope for the bigger projects.

Materials

6 mm or 8 mm offcuts of
    unbleached cotton rope
General sewing kit
Key ring blanks
Selection of thread colors

Techniques

Block stitch

Flat tassel finish

Key Rings

Method

The technique for these is simple. Take your rope offcut (anything over 7.8 in. / 20 cm will work) and start your spiral **(1–10)**. When you have about 3 in. (8 cm) left on your offcut, secure your stitch by using a small section of block stitch and take your work off the machine.

Let's use the flat tassel technique to finish the key ring.

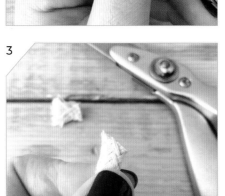

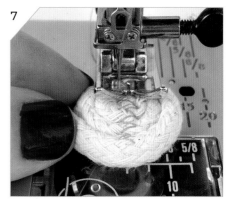

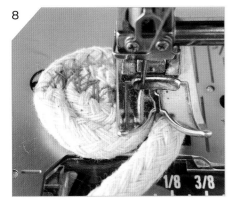

8

9

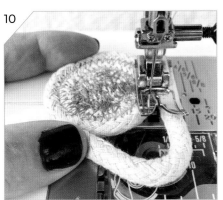

10

11

12

13

Flat-Tassel-Finish Technique

Thread the key ring blank through the rope and push it against the block stitching **(11)**. Carefully push the whole piece back under the machine, and block-stitch the loose rope to the spiral to secure the key ring. Leave 0.8 in. (2 cm) of rope unstitched for the tassel.

Take your key ring off the machine, and lay it on a flat surface **(12)**. Use a pin or a tapestry needle to unbraid the loose rope. Be sure to turn it over, and make sure you catch all of the braid. The block stitching you have done will keep the integrity of the work, so really go for it and unbraid the fibers all the way to the stitching **(13)**. Trim with sharp scissors to create a neat edge.

Your key ring is ready to use—why not make a few and keep them as handy gifts?

Trinket Dish Duo

Here we go! This is the first project where you will stitch a 3-D shape. These trinket dishes are quick and satisfying to make and are a great way to utilize your new artisan ropework skills to make your first 3-D objects.

Materials

10 ft. (3 m) × 6 mm,
    unbleached cotton rope (per dish)
Bright thread color
General sewing kit
Neutral thread color

Techniques

Block stitch
Loop finish

Trinket Dish Duo

Method

Stitch a starting spiral of 2.7 in. (7 cm) in your neutral thread (**1–2**).

To create the 3-D dish, you need to know how to "build shape." Refer to the "Getting Started" chapter on p. 18 for full detailed information.

In short, to build shape you simply change the angle of the spiral, so the thread is connecting the loose rope to a different point in the spiral (**3**). Use your left hand to support the spiral from underneath and angle it up toward the presser foot. Remember, the sharper the angle you make with your left hand, the steeper your spiral will be.

For these dishes, you are aiming for a shallow but defined shape (**4**). Concentrate on your left hand doing the shaping work by holding the spiral from underneath; meanwhile, your right hand keeps the loose rope taut but flowing through the

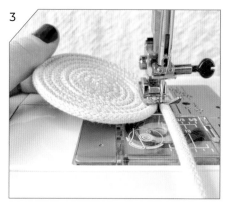

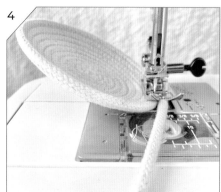

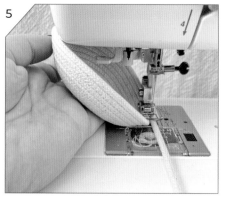

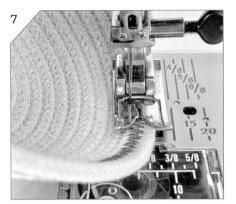

7

8

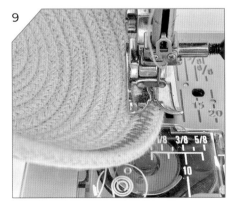

9

10

machine. Remember—every stitch that connects the loose rope to the spiral grows the spiral.

Stitch one round and then let go with both hands to see if the spiral is holding the new angle. You should see that the round you've just stitched is sitting "proud" on top of the previous spiral, rather than next to it (i.e., flat).

If it's still flat, try again. Pull the spiral up a little harder. It can take a couple of goes to feel where it needs to be, and how much tension you need to

hold in both your hands, but once you have it, it will feel easy (5). Once you've managed a couple of rounds, you can pull up a little harder with your left hand to keep the shape building (6). Keep stitching until you have 9.8 in. (25 cm) of rope left.

Switch over to your brightly colored thread and stitch halfway around the dish until there's just enough rope left to make a loop (7–9). Create a line of block stitching that goes halfway back around the dish. Then finish your dish with the same loop technique from the Mats and Coasters project.

Repeat to make your second dish and then sit back to admire your first 3-D artisan ropework pieces (10).

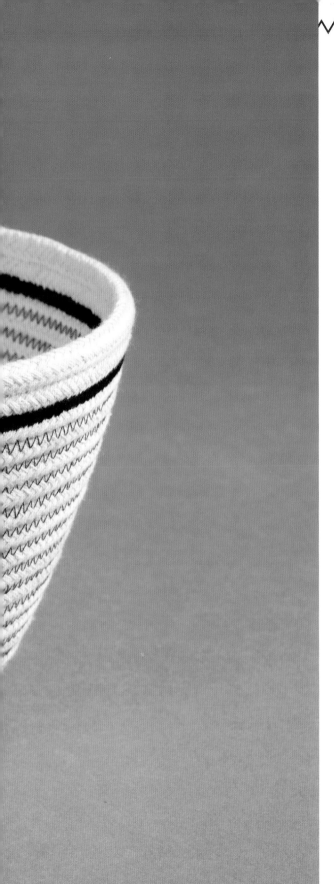

Tassel Bowl

This is the first of three projects working with a 33 ft. (10 m) rope length. The aim is to focus on building a classic bowl shape. For this reason, stick with one color to allow you to concentrate solely on the shape.

Materials

33 ft. (10 m) × 8 mm,
    unbleached cotton rope
Blue thread
General sewing kit

Techniques

Block stitch
Knotted tassel finish

Tassel Bowl

Method

Stitch a starting spiral of 3.5 in. (9 cm) **(1)**.

Building shape: move your left hand underneath your spiral and lift to create an angle **(2)**. This time you are aiming to grow the spiral *outward and upward*. Work with your machine as you stitch, so the shape works easily with the side of your sewing machine.

At first you will be able to use your pinkie and ring finger to guide the shape **(3)**. As the spiral grows, your hand will naturally move farther away, and your left hand will be supporting the spiral from the base of the work. While you're stitching, keep in mind that the angle is created at the point where the *spiral and loose rope connect* at the needle **(4–6)**. Focus your efforts on what is happening there, while also supporting the spiral.

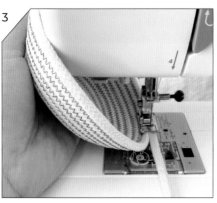

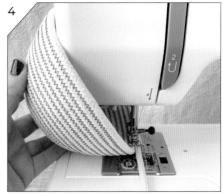

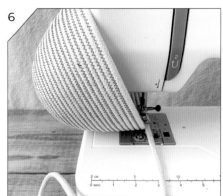

TIP: It's not a problem if your bobbin runs out before you get to the end of the spiral. This will certainly occur in larger projects. Just switch your bobbin and use a small section of block stitch to resecure the thread. Allow the loose thread to travel around while you stitch your next round, then trim away with snips before it goes back under the machine. This saves a lot of messing around trying to find the thread under the machine and stops it from causing tangles later.

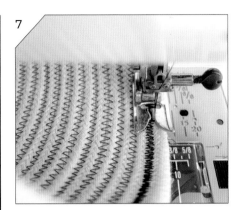

Keep building the shape all the way until you are left with 3.9 in. (10 cm) of rope **(7–10)**. To add a bit of interest, create a longer line of block stitch by reverse stitching for half a round. Stitch forward again and take off the machine.

Let's finish your bowl with a variation of a tassel finish.

Knotted-Tassel-Finish Technique

Take the end of the rope and loop it around itself **(11)**. Push the end through the loop and pull to create a knot. Do this as tightly as possible to your last stitch to create a neat finish.

Place the rope on a flat surface and use a straight pin or tapestry needle to unbraid it **(12)**. Remember to check underneath to make sure you catch all the fibers. Finish by using a sharp pair of scissors to create a neat edge.

Now your first 33 ft. (10 m) project is complete, and you have achieved one of the most wonderful shapes in artisan ropework. You are well practiced and can tackle the next project with confidence.

Looped Cone

This is the first project that may present you with some challenges; hence the tongue-in-cheek materials. The reason for this is because you will be working *against* the shape of your sewing machine to create the piece; plus it will feel a bit counter to what you've already learned. Usually, it's all about finding flow and stitching in a rhythm, but this project is more stop-start. Making cones is tricky business with domestic sewing machines, but I have perfected a technique that means you can give it your best shot with a good chance of success.

Please note that I have deliberately included quite a few thread changes in this design to give you the opportunity to take the work off the machine and check your progress. If you find yourself in flow and you don't want to stop stitching—then keep going! The thread changes are purely aesthetic, and it will not affect the structure of the design if you choose to stay with one color.

Before you start stitching, give your sewing machine a really good clean above the presser foot and under the machine's arm. This is because your spiral will come into contact with these areas, and cotton is easily stained by old oil or greasy fluff.

Materials

33 ft. (10 m) × 8 mm,
    unbleached cotton rope
Blue thread
General sewing kit
Neutral thread
+ a ton of patience!

Techniques

Block stitch
Fully stitched finish
Long loop

Looped Cone

Method

Building Shape

This time, building shape needs to start almost immediately after securing the spiral **(1–3)**. To do this, use the index and middle finger on your left hand to pull the spiral up as sharply as you can. You will quickly find as you stitch that bits of the presser foot impede you and make continuing the angle difficult. Don't worry. Keep stitching slowly and steadily until your spiral can go over the top of these bits **(4)**. Aim to complete seven rounds before switching to the neutral thread.

To maintain the angle you have started, you will need to do something that is counterintuitive to what you have learned already **(5)**. Instead of pulling up from underneath with your left hand, you need to squash and guide the spiral through the machine **(6)**. You might find you can stitch half a round and then you need to stop and pull the

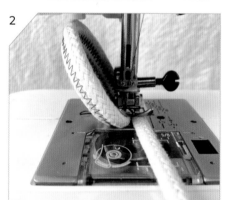

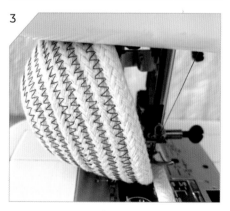

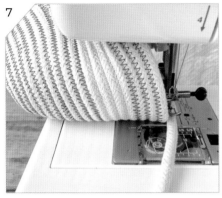

spiral back through the machine to continue stitching. The main thing is to make sure that the loose rope is meeting and connecting to the spiral.

Change the thread back to blue after three or four rounds **(7)**. Continue to use this "squash and stitch" technique for a further four or five rounds.

Now the spiral should have grown wide enough that you can continue to build the shape with it angled on the outside of the sewing machine, instead of underneath **(8)**. The angle will be a bit wider, but if you guide it with your left hand it should be comfortable to stitch.

Change thread every five rounds or so, until you have 3.3 ft. (1 m) of rope left. Finish here with a section of block stitch and take the spiral off the machine.

Long-Loop Technique

This cone is designed to hang from a hook on a long loop **(9)**. To make the loop, leave a gap of 1.9 in. (5 cm) from the point where you have just block-stitched.

Measure a 15.7 in. (40 cm) length of the loose rope and leave this unstitched—this will become the loop. Reconnect the rope from the 15.7 in. (40 cm) mark with block stitch and then stitch a final round to the base of the loop.

To finish your cone, let's use the fully stitched technique.

Fully Stitched Finish Technique

Secure the rope with a few stitches and then take it off the machine **(10–11)**. Use a pair of sharp scissors to trim away as much of the excess rope as you can. Then put it back under the machine and slowly stitch over the area again and again until it is completely covered in thread.

In my experience, this is the most likely point at which your needle might snap or warp, so stitch slowly and take your time. It is wise to change your needle every few ropework projects, because the needle does blunt quickly from the repeated effort of punching through the thick fibers.

If you made it through this 33 ft. (10 m) project, I sincerely offer you my heartiest congratulations **(12)**. Hang your Looped Cone somewhere in pride of place and fill it with beautiful dried flowers, safe in the knowledge that you have completed the only project where I ask you to work against your sewing machine.

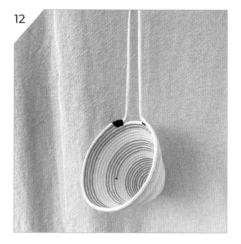

Technicolor Tray

This is the last of the 33 ft. (10 m) projects and a return to a wider spiral. This project is intended to get you thinking about color and design.

Materials

33 ft. (10 m) × 6 mm,
    unbleached cotton rope
General sewing kit
Neutral thread
Threads: four shades of blue

Techniques

Block stitch
Flat tassel finish

Technicolor Tray

Method

This time you are making an almost flat spiral, but with the thinner 6 mm rope (1–2). This thinner rope can be trickier to keep flat, so concentrate on keeping it flat with your left hand, and watch the angle that is happening at the point of the needle to stop the shape from building before you are ready.

Aside from creating a neat flat spiral, the most important element of this project is choosing the color palette and deciding what order you want your colors to appear (3–4). This time I worked with an all-blue palette and graduated the color from light to dark at the edge.

Consider how you would like the finished tray to appear, and decide on your palette—for this size, you have space for up to four thread colors. If you have enough bobbins, fill them before you start so you can do quick thread changes while you're working.

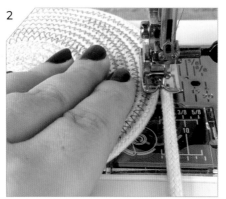

These are the points that I changed color on the flat spiral:

Neutral to 1.2 in. (3 cm)
Very light blue to 1.9 in. (5 cm)
Light blue to 4.7 in. (12 cm)
Blue to 7.8 in. (20 cm)

Building Shape

After 7.8 in. (20 cm) of flat spiral, it's time to build the shape (5–6). This is a short, sharp build since you'll have only a limited length of rope left. Pull up at a hard angle, and after one round, change to your final thread color—for me, this was dark blue.

Continue to stitch on the hard angle until you get to the end (7–8). Finish your tray with the flat tassel finish from the key ring project (see p. 37).

That was the last of the 33 ft. (10 m) projects (9). It's amazing how many different objects you can make from the same length of rope. From here, the projects will build and add to the techniques that you have already learned.

7

8

9

Intermediate Projects

Now that you have completed the Beginner Projects and have practiced the fundamentals of how to make a spiral and building shape, it's time to move on to the next level of techniques. The next few projects are designed to gently engage your creative brain to get you thinking about design and give you the skills you need to start progressing in your artisan ropework journey.

Reflection Vessels

Vessels have been one of the mainstays of my practice. A vessel simply means a hollow container. For this project, you are aiming to make two of the same shape. They are called reflection vessels since the thread changes are opposite in each vessel, giving the illusion that they are a reflection of each other.

Materials

42.6 ft. (13 m) × 6 mm,
    unbleached cotton rope
    (for each vessel)
General sewing kit
Neutral thread
Yellow-toned thread

Techniques

Block stitch
Twisted loop tassel

Reflection Vessels

Method

Before you start stitching, count backward 19.6 ft. (6 m) from the end of your rope and mark it with a straight pin.

Begin with the yellow thread and make your starting spiral to 2.7 in. (7 cm) **(1)**.

Building Shape
Build the shape from 2.7 in. (7 cm) **(2)**. You are aiming to create quite a steep outward shape, which will give your vessel depth. Imagine you are a potter and are encouraging the rope to shape outward as if it were clay. Aim to get the spiral leaning against the arm of the machine, and use that angle to build from. You will need to maintain the angle throughout the vessel.

Remember to shape the work with your left hand and keep the tension of the loose rope in your right hand **(3)**.

Keep building until you hit the 19.6 ft. (6 m) marker pin **(4)**. Stitch a 1.9 in. (5 cm) line of block stitch before switching to your neutral thread. Yellow can appear quite pale on the rope, and adding this small line of block color really draws the eye and shows off the yellow.

Continue building with the neutral thread **(5–6)**. Don't be afraid to push the spiral against the arm of the machine to maintain your angle. Keep stitching until you have 7.8 in. (20 cm) of rope left.

To finish these vessels, let's use a variation on the loop technique—a twisted loop tassel.

Twisted-Loop Tassel Technique

Instead of pushing the end of the rope into the vessel and stitching it into place, you are going to create a loop and then have a loose piece of rope that flows down perpendicular to the vessel **(7)**. Stitch it down firmly

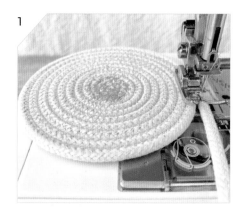

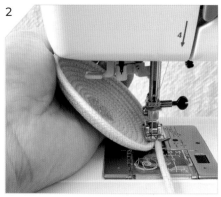

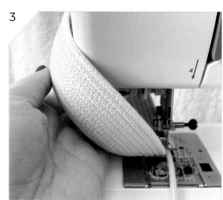

4

5

6
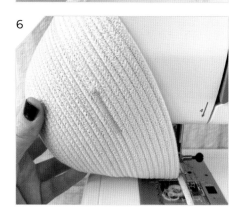

7
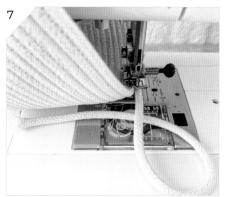

8
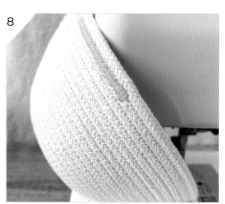

9

with block stitch and then take it off the machine. Tassel-finish the loose rope, then trim to make it neat. This way you get the lovely loop, but the added texture of the tassel draws the eye to the height of the vessel.

Make your second vessel following all the same steps, but reverse the thread changes and start with your neutral thread **(8)**. When you switch to yellow at the 19.6 ft. (6 m) marker, still do the line of block stitch in yellow rather than neutral, so that both vessels match in the same place.

Making multiples of the same shape is a great way to hone your skills, and these vessels are ready to serve as useful and beautiful objects in your living space **(9)**. For instance, they would make an ideal home for cacti on your windowsill. Try experimenting with different colour combinations, see pages 118 and 122 for inspiration.

Jewelry Holder

Gap sections are an easy but essential technique in artisan ropework. Making this jewelry holder will give you plenty of practice to master it, and the result will be a useful home for your favorite dangly earrings and pins.

Materials

39 ft. (12 m) × 6 mm,
    unbleached cotton rope
General sewing kit
Neutral thread

Techniques

Block stitch

Gap sections

Twisted loop

Jewelry Holder

Method

Make your starting spiral to 3.9 in. (10 cm) **(1)**. This design is a fully flat spiral, with gap sections placed at intervals across the spiral. Let's look at this technique in more detail.

Gap Sections Technique

Gap sections are essential in designs such as bags, where you need to leave space to add handles, or on baskets where you want to add a hanging section **(2)**. For this design, you are aiming to make small sections that are just big enough to hang jewelry through.

A gap section is created when the rope is not stitched directly to the spiral but is secured either side with a small section of block stitch **(3)**.

To make a gap, block-stitch where you want the gap to start. The more stitching you do, the stronger your gap will be. Then, gently pull away the loose rope with your right hand and stitch along the spiral without allowing the loose rope to attach. Once you've reached the correct width for your gap, reintroduce your loose rope and block-stitch to resecure it to the spiral.

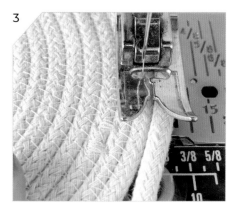

4

For this design, the gap sections need to be quite small—between 0.4 and 0.5 in. (1–1.5 cm) **(4)**—since the gaps are intended as spaces for earrings to hang, and brooches or pins to be poked through and secured. The more gap sections you add on this spiral, the more jewelry you will be able to hang from it.

Try to make your gaps equal—it's easy to get in a rhythm and eyeball the width of your sections, or to count the number of stitches you do when the loose rope is pulled away, to make the gaps equal. Keep stitching and making gaps until you have 3.3 ft. (1 m) of rope left.

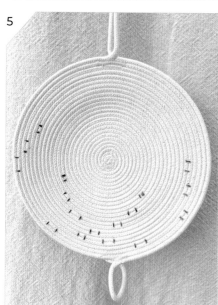

5

From the point where you reach 3.9 in. (10 cm) in spiral width, you can start adding gap sections. Aim to add a new section on every round and try to stagger them so that your jewelry will hang from different points of the spiral. I made seventeen gap sections in total, and they covered the bottom two-thirds of the spiral **(5)**. It felt like a lot of sections when I was stitching, but afterward I actually wished I'd added in more! So feel free to really go for it and put plenty of gaps in the spiral.

With this last piece of rope, you need to add two loops—a large one at the top and a smaller one at the bottom. Use a variation on the loop technique to achieve this.

6

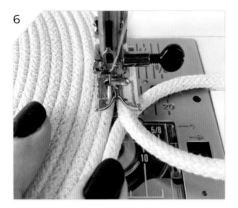

7

8

Twisted-Loop Technique

This is a simple variation on the loop technique from the Looped Cone project (see p. 52) **(6–8)**. Instead of making a gap and resecuring the loose rope, create a loop and twist it so that it looks like half a figure eight. There's no need to leave a gap—make the loop, twist it, and secure it with block stitch before continuing.

Use a ruler to mark where the second loop should be placed **(9)**. It needs to be exactly opposite the first loop. Stitch until you reach that point, then create a smaller version of the first twisted loop.

Finish the spiral after making the second loop. Tuck the loose rope underneath the spiral and stitch it down well.

9

Now that you have completed the jewelry holder, you have a place to hang your earrings—and you have had plenty of gap section practice that will serve you well for the projects to come.

Hanging Basket

Hanging baskets are one of those wonderful objects that you can find a use for in any room of the house. This design is a modern take on 1970s macramé and utilizes the gap section technique from the Jewelry Holder project.

Materials

36 ft. (11 m) × 6 mm,
　　unbleached cotton rope
15 ft. (4.5 m) × 3 mm,
　　unbleached cotton rope
General sewing kit
Green thread
Neutral thread
Wide washer or metal loop

Techniques

Block stitch
Gap sections
Fully stitched finish

Hanging Basket

Method

Before you start stitching, count backward 6.5 ft. (2 m) from the end of your rope and mark it with a pin.

Begin with the green thread and make your starting spiral to 2.4 in. (6 cm) **(1)**.

Building Shape

The shape you are aiming to build is an outward curve, which maintains an outward angle for the whole basket **(2)**.

Work with your sewing-machine arm by allowing the spiral to grow outward, until you can use the arm of the machine to help you support the shape **(3)**.

Use your left hand to gently encourage the spiral to spin and flow through the machine, while you use the sewing-machine arm to help you guide the shape. You'll be amazed at how quickly the spiral will build if you can get into a flow. Remember to keep the loose rope in your right hand taut, but continually flowing through the machine.

Stitch all the way up to the 6.5 ft. (2 m) marker pin in one thread color (I chose green) and finish with a small section of block stitch **(4)**. Take your work off the machine—it's time to add your gap sections.

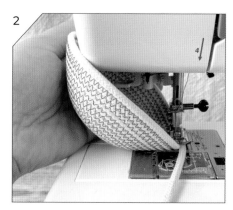

Adding Gap Sections

For this design, you will need to create three gap sections **(5)**. The gaps don't need to be very wide because the rope you are putting through them is only 0.12 in. (3 mm), but aim to make them 1.2 in. (3 cm) to give yourself plenty of wiggle room. The first gap section will be where you have just finished stitching **(6)**. Use a ruler to measure a V shape from the first gap, and use straight pins to mark where the other two sections will go. Essentially, you're splitting the basket into thirds.

Put your work back under the machine and stitch the three gap sections (refer to the Jewelry Holder project for full gap section instructions, p. 66) **(7)**. Remember to block-stitch either side of the gaps to make them extra strong. Once you have completed all three gaps, continue stitching until you reach the end of the rope **(8–9)**. Use the fully stitched technique from the Looped Cone project to finish your spiral (see p. 52).

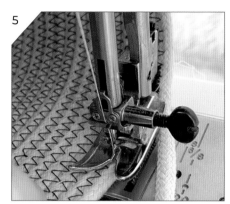

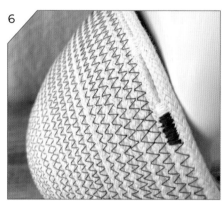

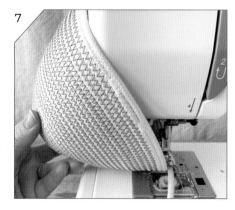

Adding the Hanging Section

To make the hanging section of the basket, take your 15 ft. (4.5 m) of 3 mm rope **(10)** and cut it into three equal sections **(11)**. Put one piece of rope through each of your gap sections and make sure all the ends are equal.

Have your metal loop/washer within easy reach. Turn the basket upside down, so the ropes hang toward the ground. Gather the ropes from the middle with your other hand and slide your fingers down so the ropes sit in the middle and are held taut.

Flip the basket back over and hold the ropes up. The ropes should now be equally distributed, and you can slip the washer/loop through the top of the ropes.

There are lots of ways that you can secure the ropes, using different macramé knot techniques **(12–15)**. The way I do it is to split the ropes into two groups of three. Next, I pull them back around the loop and do a basic knot to secure them. Then I put the two groups of rope back through the loop and tie them twice on the other side as tightly as I can manage. Finally, I trim them short. Alternatively, you can unbraid them for a tassel effect.

Your hanging basket is ready to be a home to air plants and cacti, or as a useful place to keep garlic in the kitchen.

Foraging Basket

I was out on a lovely long walk around my local area, and there were some beautiful flowers in the hedgerows. I wished that I had something with me that I could gather this nature into. As soon as I got home, I came up with this design.

This basket is essentially a large spiral, but with handles and lots of thread detail to create interest. I've included a loop finish that gives you the option to attach your floristry snips, so you'll be all set for any gardening adventures.

Materials

82 ft. (25 m) × 6 mm,
    unbleached cotton rope
3 shades of green thread
General sewing kit

Techniques

Block stitch
Handles
Loop finish

Foraging Basket

Method

Alternate your green threads and stitch a flat spiral to 14.5 in. (37 cm) **(1)**. The thread changes I used were

· light green to 5 in. (13 cm)
· dark green to 7.8 in. (20 cm)
· medium green to 10.6 in. (27 cm)
· light green to 13 in. (33 cm)
· dark green to 14.5 in. (37 cm)

On each thread change, do a line of block stitching that covers two-thirds of the last round **(2–4)**. This will make the colors much more effective, and it will also give your foraging basket a stronger structure for longevity.

Once you have reached 14.5 in. (37 cm), it's time to create the handles **(5)**. Take your work off the machine and measure a gap section of 7 in. (18 cm) from where you have just finished stitching. Find the middle of the section (at 3.9 in. / 9 cm) and use your ruler to go

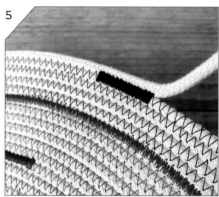

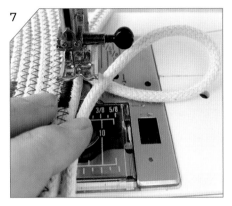

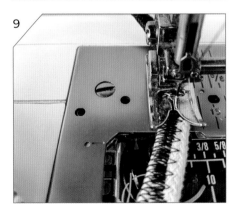

straight across the middle of the spiral to the other side. Measure another section of 7 in. (18 cm). This is where the handles will go. Mark out the sections with straight pins.

Block-stitch at the point of the first section and then pull away the loose rope and stitch down just the spiral until you reach the 7 in. (18 cm) marker pin. Keep your needle in the spiral and use your ruler to measure a 11.8 in. (30 cm) length of the loose rope. Reattach the 11.8 in. (30 cm) point to the end of the gap section with block stitch and continue stitching. Repeat the process on the other side to create two handles.

Stitch a final round so that both handles are made with two sections of rope (6). Make a loop at the bottom of the second handle and stitch it down firmly (7–8). Trim away any excess rope and fully stitch down any loose fibers.

Now go back over your last round with a thick line of block stitch. When you reach the handles, block-stitch the underside of them (9). This will take some time, so go steady and make sure all the rope is covered. This will make the handles extra strong, and it will also look effective.

Your foraging basket is ready to accompany you on many happy outdoor adventures.

> **TIP:** If you're finding it difficult to keep the spiral flat, and your sewing machine sits on top of a table, try putting a stack of hardcover books next to your machine to extend your work area. This way, it's easier to control the spiral with your left hand and to keep your right hand working on the rope tension.

Vase Vessel

This vessel is a departure from the other projects, since the idea is to create a shape for an already existing object. I chose a plain, stubby vase that I wanted to sit inside a rope vessel. In this exercise I'll show you the process I used to create the right shape for this project. Choose an object of your own at home and then follow the steps to see if you can make your own rope vessel for it.

Materials

8 mm, unbleached cotton rope (length determined by your chosen shape)

General sewing kit

Neutral threads in a couple of shades

Techniques

Block stitch

Flat tassel finish

Vase Vessel

Method

Make a Plan

The first step with this project is to measure your chosen object and make a plan for your starting spiral and vessel shape aims **(1)**.

The vase I wanted to cover measured

- 4 in. (10.5 cm) width at the base
- 5.5 in. (14 cm) width at the top **(2)**
- 5 in. (13 cm) high **(3)**

I know from these measurements that to make my vase sit inside the vessel, the base will have to be at least 4 in. (10.5 cm) across. This dictates that my starting spiral must be 4 in. or wider.

The width of the vase is 5.5 in. (14 cm) at the top, which means I need to make sure my vessel is *at least* as wide as this at the top. This tells me that I need to allow the shape to grow outward as well as upward to accommodate the full width of the vase.

The height is 5 in. (13 cm), and I know that if I make it exactly this height, the vase will be visible sitting inside the vessel. I want to add a little extra length to make the vase disappear inside its custom-made rope home.

I have the benefit of a lot of experience in working with rope lengths, so I estimated that 65.6 ft. (20 m) would be plenty of rope to create the shape. I suggest you allow yourself a generous pile of rope to work with, so that you can sew freely and not worry about running out halfway through your project, which can be very frustrating.

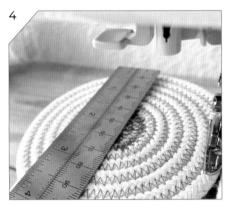

4

My aim is to create a vessel that will bring a different textural element to the vase, but the flowers will be the main event, so I chose to work with a neutral color palette. I opted for

- light gray
- neutral
- whispy gray

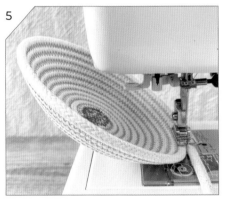

5

My other aim was to try to keep all my thread changes in one line on the vessel, so that they can be hidden around the back to give it as clean a look as possible. I decided in advance that I would do a block stitch finish with a very short, flat tassel.

6

Stitching

I stitched a starting spiral to 4.3 in. (11 cm) and then built the shape from there (**4–6**). I stitched eight rounds in light-gray thread before switching to the whispy gray. Then I stitched another five rounds in this thread before switching to the final neutral color.

The thread changes gave me the opportunity to check on the width, so I knew about halfway up that I needed to stop going outward since the width had grown to 7 in. (18 cm) **(7–11)**. If it went out anymore, it might become too wide for the vase and not hide it **(12–14)**.

I decided to aim to keep building the height up and then to bring the vessel over the machine to try to narrow the width for the last few rounds of the spiral.

My finished vessel was

- 4.3 in. (11 cm) at the base
- 6.7 in. (17 cm) at the top
(but 7in. / 18 cm around the middle)
- 6.3 in. (16 cm) high

To show off the finished result, I put a ball of chicken wire in the base of the vase and arranged a lovely big bunch of dried flowers in there. This now sits proudly on my mantelpiece.

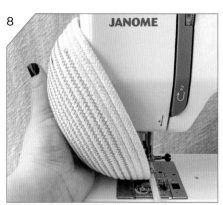

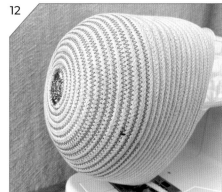

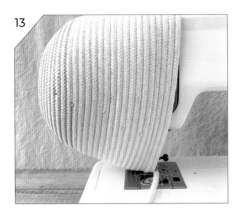

13

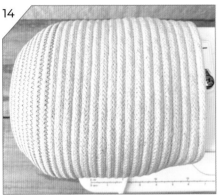

14

I hope you will be inspired to make a rope vessel for a vase or pot in your home. A really useful starting point is to take the measurements from an existing object and apply them to your own projects.

Advanced Projects

Well done on all your hard work so far! Now that you are well and truly familiar with all the fundamental skills and are comfortable with spiral work, it's time to create some bigger shapes. These projects focus on helping you achieve skills such as matching handles and maintaining shape.

The final project is to make a beach bag: the perfect project to put all your new skills into practice. Once complete, it will be a beautiful and functional basket for you to enjoy and use for years to come.

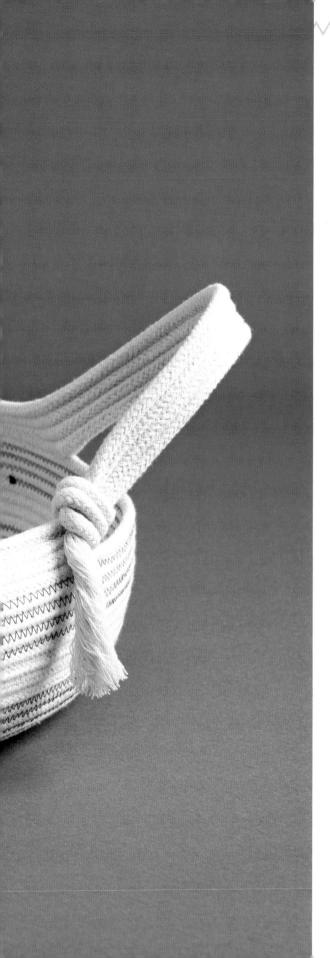

Monochrome-Handled Catchall Basket

A catchall simply means a basket that you can chuck anything into. Since it's one of the larger projects in this book, I have designed it to give you confidence in building shape with a wider spiral and handle making.

Materials

98 ft. (30 m) × 8 mm,
    unbleached cotton rope
Dark neutral thread (e.g., gray/black)
General sewing kit
Neutral thread

Techniques

Block stitch
Handles
Wrapped tassel finish

Monochrome-Handled Catchall Basket

Method

Before you start, mark 16.4 ft. (5 m) from the end with a straight pin. This marks the position where you'll make the handles.

Make a starting spiral of 11.8 in. (30 cm) **(1)**. To add interest, change your thread colors as you go. I changed threads at

- neutral to 7.5 in. (19 cm)
- black to 9.4 in. (24 cm)
- neutral to 11 in. (28 cm)
- black to 11.8 in. (30 cm)

Building Shape

For this basket, you are aiming to create a curved shape that goes out and then comes in again from the point of the handles **(2)**. To get started, support the spiral from underneath with your left hand and bring the angle up, so that as you stitch the spiral is growing outward and upward **(3)**.

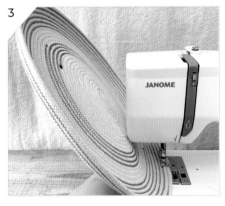

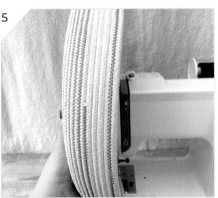

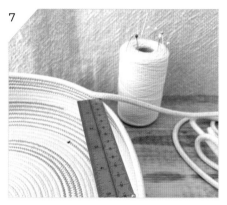

7

8

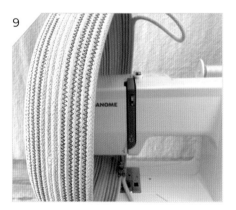

9

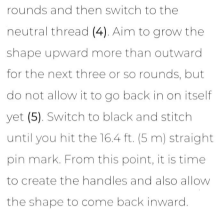

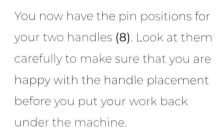

Stitch on this angle for about three rounds and then switch to the neutral thread **(4)**. Aim to grow the shape upward more than outward for the next three or so rounds, but do not allow it to go back in on itself yet **(5)**. Switch to black and stitch until you hit the 16.4 ft. (5 m) straight pin mark. From this point, it is time to create the handles and also allow the shape to come back inward.

Creating Handles

Take your work off the machine and measure 5.9 in. (15 cm) from the point that you've just finished stitching **(6)**. Use a straight pin to mark it. Now, spin the basket so that the gap section you've just measured is around the other side and facing you **(7)**. Use a ruler to find the middle of the section (which will be 2.9 in. / 7.5 cm in this case) and then hold the ruler straight down the middle of the basket to the other side that is now in front of you. Be sure to go through the center of

your spiral to make it symmetrical. Now you have the middle of your opposite handle. Measure 2.9 in. (7.5 cm) on each side from that point and mark with straight pins.

You now have the pin positions for your two handles **(8)**. Look at them carefully to make sure that you are happy with the handle placement before you put your work back under the machine.

Switch to your neutral thread and block-stitch a section over the black where you finished stitching. Now pull the loose rope away so it is not being stitched to the spiral, and carefully stitch along your gap section until you reach the pin marker. Keep the needle in the spiral and lift the presser foot.

To make your handles even, you need to use exactly the same amount of rope for each one **(9)**. To do this, take your ruler and measure the loose rope from the point that it disconnects at the gap section, and carefully pull it taut so you can measure 9.8 in. (25 cm). Reconnect the loose rope at that 9.8 in. point by encouraging the rope back under the presser foot and securing it with block stitch.

That's the first handle connected. Before continuing, remember you are aiming to get the shape to start curving in on itself, so as you continue stitching around to the next straight pin marker, use your left hand to pull the basket over the top of the machine while you stitch. When you hit the next straight pin, it's time to make your second handle. Repeat the handle-making process.

With the last few feet of rope, you are aiming to build your handles and keep bringing the spiral shape inward **(10)**. Stitch slowly and use your left hand to pull the spiral over the sewing machine, at the same time as steadying the loose rope with your right hand.

You will need to shape the handles on your second round after starting them **(11)**. At this point the handle is just a single piece of loose rope that's been stitched to the spiral. To give the handles form, they need to be stitched over several times.

When you reach the first handle, use your right hand to guide the two loose ropes together **(12)**. Allow the basket, with your left hand, to move off its current angle, to allow you to stitch the handle shape. You are aiming for an upside-down U shape.

Shape the rope upward as you stitch, and then once you hit the middle of the handle, change the angle so you are stitching back down toward the spiral. It's not necessary to do any further block stitching, so continue to stitch as before when you reach the main spiral and continue to pull it over the machine to create the curve.

10

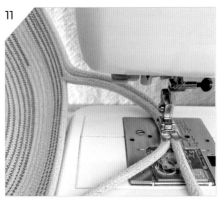

11

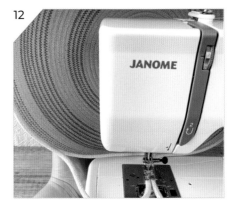

12

Repeat when you get to the second handle **(13)**. You should have enough rope to go around three times in total, and it becomes easier each time as the formwork is set. End your stitching on the end of the second handle if possible **(14)**. Then block-stitch and remove from the machine.

You could finish with any of the techniques from the previous projects, but I'm going to show you my favorite way to finish a handled basket.

Wrapped-Tassel-Finish Technique

Wrap the rope up the handle three times and then guide the end back through all three loops **(15–17)**. Pull tightly and tassel the end. It's a simple but effective technique.

Now that you have completed this Catchall Basket, your practice with working with larger spirals is well underway.

Basket with Natural-Wood Handle

This is a great project to do before you attempt the Beach Bag. Its deep, rounded shape creates a satisfying basket that you will love for years to come. You may already have a piece of driftwood that's been waiting for a project like this, but if not, take the opportunity to go for a nice long walk in a park or a wood and forage a stick that can work as a handle.

Materials
82 ft. (25 m) × 8 mm, unbleached cotton rope
Bright thread
General sewing kit
Piece of driftwood or foraged stick, for the handle

Techniques
Block stitch
Gap sections
Loops

Basket with Natural-Wood Handle

Method

Before you start stitching, count backward 10 ft. (3 m) from the end of the rope and mark it with a straight pin or safety pin.

For the project photography I made this in teal, but I also tried this design in black and neutral, and the two baskets have a very different aesthetic. By now you will likely have started to realize your own color preferences with the rope, so feel free to choose colors that really appeal to you.

Make your starting spiral to 7.8 in. (20 cm). Remember to continue to focus on keeping the angle flat at the point where the spiral and loose rope join **(1)**.

Building Shape
To build the shape, you are aiming to create an immediately steep angle that has a slight outward trajectory **(2)**. This means that your spiral will gain depth quickly, but the gentle curved angle will prevent it from getting stuck on your machine **(3)**. Aim to work in harmony with the machine shape, so that the process of stitching feels pleasant and flowing. If the angle is too straight, you may find that it will be a battle to keep the shape building against the machine.

It is very likely you will run out of thread somewhere along the way on this larger spiral **(4)**. Refill your bobbin and use block stitch to get going again. You could even do a longer line of block stitch to add some extra stitch detail if you wish.

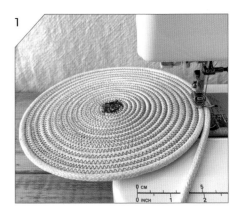

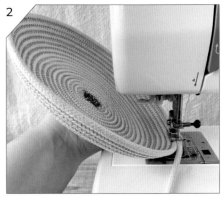

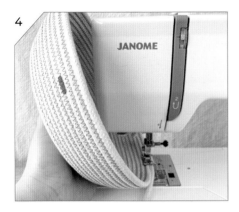

4

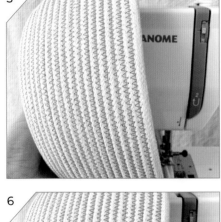

5

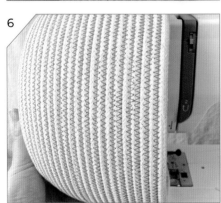

6

Stitch on the same steep but curved angle all the way up to your 10 ft. (3 m) straight pin mark **(5–6)**.

The next step is to create two loops that the wooden handle can sit through **(7)**. The loops are essentially a variation on the gap sections. (Refer back to the Hanging Basket project on p. 72 for full details on gap sections if you need a refresher.)

These loops need to be *directly opposite* each other so the handle will sit straight across the basket **(8)**.

Use your ruler to go straight across the basket from the first gap, and use a straight pin to mark the gap on the opposite side. The width of your section will depend entirely on how thick your piece of wood is. Make sure there is enough space to get your handle in, but aim for the fit to be snug so the wood stays put once it's in and doesn't slip out.

7

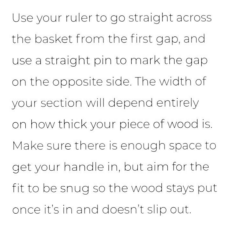

8

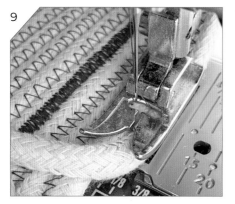

9

10

11

The variation is very simple. Pull the loose rope away as normal after the first block stitch. When you reattach it, leave a longer section of the rope out in the gap. This will be the loop, so however much you leave in relation to the width of the gap will be your loop size. It is essentially a small version of the handles in the Monochrome-Handled Catchall Basket project (see p. 90).

Once you've stitched both loops in place, continue stitching and take care to follow the loop shape with each round (9). Stitch these last few rounds on a tight pulling-in angle—where the basket may come over the top of your machine. This will make the top of the basket angle inward to finish the curved shape.

To finish this basket, I used the fully stitched technique, but it would look equally good with a knotted tassel.

Now that your basket is finished, simply place the wood handle between the loops and your basket is ready to use (10–11).

Wall Hanging: Rope and Clay

This project is a little different from the others in this book. It is to create an unusual wall hanging out of rope and clay to brighten up your walls. There are quite a few elements to making this project, and you will need to factor in drying time, so plan to make this over several days. Try to achieve the given sizes for each of the components so it all fits together, but free your creativity and explore with whatever colors and patterns speak to you to decorate the rope and clay elements.

Materials

4 pieces of 6 mm
   unbleached cotton rope:
1 16.4 ft. (5 m) long
1 3.3 ft. (1 m) long
2 29.5 in. (75 cm) long
3 mm, unbleached cotton rope, or twine
   for assembling the mural
2 colors of heat-setting textile paints
Acrylic paint pens or acrylic paint
Clay, good quality, air-drying
Neutral thread
Round cutters, in several sizes
Zinc washer

Wall Hanging: Rope and Clay

Method

CLAY ELEMENTS

Make the Clay Elements
Take the clay and roll it out until it's 0.4 in. (1 cm) thick **(1)**. If it's too thin, it will be flimsy and will break easily. Too thick, and it will be sturdy but take forever to dry.

Cut out a number of different-sized circles **(2)**. It's a really good idea to make more than you need in case of breakages, especially when assembling the mural. Also, cut some of the circles in half to make semicircles.

Using the offcuts from the clay circles, make some large clay beads. Roll the clay in your palms to make them into 3-D spheres, approximately 1.5 in. (4 cm) in circumference.

You will need to make holes in all your clay elements so they can be assembled onto the piece. Use a pencil to punch holes through the clay. For the larger full circles, punch three holes; for the smaller semicircles, punch two holes; for the beads, choose a side and go straight through the middle with your pencil.

Take care to smooth the edges of the punched holes on both sides, and make sure to clear any jagged clay from inside the holes, so the rope can easily pass through.

Put the clay pieces somewhere warm to dry. Try not to put it in direct sunlight, since this can cause cracking if it dries too fast. I made these in the middle of winter, and it took three days for them to fully dry. During this time, I flipped them every day to stop the edges curling up as they dried.

Decorating the Clay
Acrylic paint is the obvious choice for decorating the clay. I used paint pens—they are really fun to use, but standard acrylic paint applied with a paintbrush is equally effective.

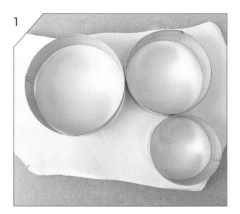

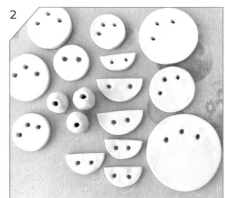

I settled on an abstract apple tree theme for my piece. I used a black paint pen to make tree trunk lines on the biggest clay circle and incorporated the holes to look like tree knots by filling them in with black paint. Once they were dry, I used a gold paint pen to highlight sections of the tree lines.

For the semicircles, I created a very simple, irregular spot design in black and gold. I left the clay beads undecorated, since I wanted them to add a sense of minimalism into the piece.

Seeing all the clay pieces together fully decorated and ready to go gives you a real idea about how your finished artwork is going to look.

You can choose any theme you want and use simple graphic patterns (as I did) to convey it. Or, if you have a gift for painting, you could do some detailed work to make the work stand out. The clay provides a blank canvas, so you can choose to decorate it however you wish.

ROPE ELEMENTS

Make the Rope Elements
There are four rope elements to this mural:

1 large spiral
16.5 ft. / 5 m long
2 small rope coins
29.5 in. / 75 cm long
1 medium rope coin
3.3 ft. / 1 m long

For the Coins
Stitch a flat spiral until you have just enough rope left to create two gap sections on the last round (**3**). The sections need to be directly opposite each other so they sit flat when connected to other parts of the mural. Use the fully stitched technique to make sure all the fibers are secured.

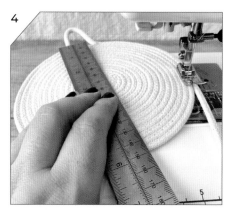

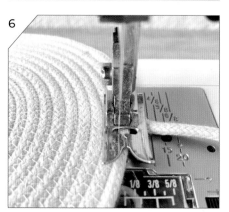

For the Large Spiral

Stitch a flat spiral until you have 4.9 ft. (1.5 m) of rope left. Create a gap section that is 1.2 in. (3 cm) wide and secured either side with block stitch. Leave enough rope loose to create a loop that is 1.4 in. (3.5 cm) high.

At this point, use a ruler to go straight down the spiral from the middle of the gap section to the other side, and mark it with a straight pin **(4–5)**. From that point, mark another point 2 in. (5 cm) apart on either side. You should now have three straight pins that will become the three gap sections on the bottom of the spiral. Stitch until you are 0.4 in. (1 cm) away from your first pin **(6)**. Make a gap section about 1 in. (2.5 cm) wide and repeat for all three pins.

To finish the spiral, stitch back up and around the loop and end at the bottom of the loop **(7–8)**. Stitch the fibers down behind the spiral so they are hidden.

Your four rope elements are ready to be decorated (9).

Decorating the Rope Elements

A note about paint—when working with a cotton rope, you can treat it as you would a cotton T-shirt in terms of paint. In other words, choose a high-quality textile paint that is set by heat. This means you paint as normal, then once it's dry, you can either iron it or steam it to fix the paint. I prefer to use a handheld steamer with rope because the steam can penetrate the in-between sections and set all of the paint. If your iron has a steam setting, I highly recommend utilizing this. But be careful not to let your iron plate touch the paint—use greaseproof paper as protection.

To fit with my abstract apple tree theme, I went for a two-tone color palette of dark green and black for the rope elements. Of course, you need to choose a color palette that suits your own theme—and don't feel limited to a two-tone either; if you want to use every color, then go for it!

I decided to use both colors on the large spiral and then do the two smallest coins in green and the largest coin in black.

Painting spiral work is very different from painting on canvas or clay (10): it's hard to do very detailed work because of the 3-D nature of the spiral. You have to work the paint in between and over the zigzag stitching, and make sure it catches all sides of the rope on the bits you want to be painted.

I tend to make a rough outline of where I want to paint and then use a stubbing technique as I would on a stencil, to work the paint into the rope. Use a small amount of paint initially and then build it up—this gives you the most control. I painted the dark green first and then went over the top with the black to make the two-tone circle design.

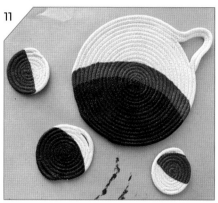

Once you have painted all your rope elements, allow them to fully dry and then either steam them or iron them to fix the paint (11).

Now all your elements are ready to be assembled into a wall mural.

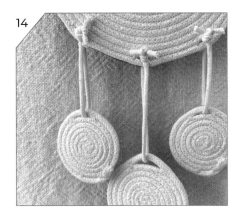

Assembly

The number of ways you can assemble your elements together is enormous—you can use one type of rope as I did, or you can use different twines on each element to add even more texture **(12)**. Experiment with adding all kinds of different macramé knots to change the look.

I will explain how I assembled my mural, and then you can use this information as a jumping-off point to assemble your own artwork.

Spread all your elements out onto a table and spend some time deciding on how you want to arrange them. My original plan was that I was going to make a fully linear design, where all the elements would be attached in a single line. However, after playing with different ideas, I settled on having three separate lines that flowed down the mural instead.

I started by using the technique from the Hanging Basket project (see p. 72) to attach the largest rope spiral to the zinc washer **(13–15)**. I used 4.9 ft. (1.5 m) of 3 mm rope, which I cut into equal sections, and then I had the knot finish at the back instead of the front. I tasseled the ends to add some extra texture.

I worked on the middle line first and decided on using just two elements to draw the eye: the largest rope coin and the painted tree trunk clay circle. To attach them, I started with the clay circle.

Using three long, equal sections of the 3 mm rope, I attached each section to a hole in the clay, then knotted these to make them sit flat. Then I wove them up through the rope coin, so that the rope would sit on the back of the coin before traveling up to the large rope spiral.

I simply knotted all the ropes together at the back of the spiral—the size of the gap section stops the ropes from slipping back through.

Then I added the two small green coins to either side of the middle line **(16)**. I just used a basic knot that I hid at the back of the main spiral.

I decided to add a semicircle clay element and a clay bead to each side—but to sit at different heights. To do this I used two long but unequal lengths of the 3 mm rope that I looped through the bottom of the coins. Then I slotted the rope through the beads and wove the rope back up and down the beads

to make them stay in place. Finally, I attached the semicircles by going through the decorated side and knotting underneath.

My mural is really just an example of what you can do with this technique. The wonderful thing about this particular project is that it's all about play. You can experiment with different-shaped clay elements or use a different fiber to create the spirals and attach them to the mural (flax or jute would create an alternative aesthetic). You can use elements from nature, such as driftwood or pine cones, to incorporate the outdoors. The options are truly limitless, and I hope that you will enjoy exploring with the rope in this alternative format.

16

Beach Bag

Now it's time to make something that can accompany you on many happy summer outings. This Beach Bag is the perfect project to utilize many of the techniques you have learned throughout this book.

Before you start, note that this is the largest spiral in the book. Your left hand may tire quickly from supporting its weight. I have deliberately included a number of thread changes in this design, so take these as an opportunity to give your hand a rest. Aim to stitch this project over a weekend, or over several sewing sessions.

Materials

164 ft. (50 m) × 8 mm,
    unbleached cotton rope
8 ft. (2.4 m) × 1.5 in. (38 mm),
    unbleached herringbone cotton tape
Bright thread and neutral thread
General sewing kit

Techniques

Adding handles
Block stitch
Gap sections
Structural stitching

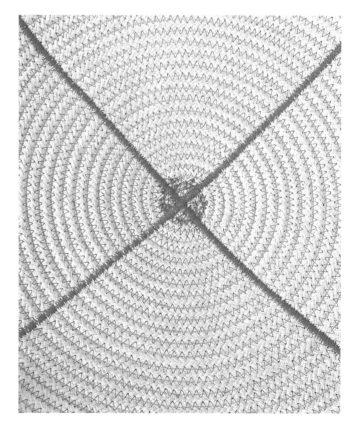

Beach Bag

Method

Start with your brightly colored thread and stitch your starting spiral to 11 in. (28 cm).

Before building the shape, it's time to add some structural stitching. Adding this in now will ensure that your bag has an extra-strong base. The stitching itself is aesthetically pleasing and will only add to the beauty of your bag.

Structural Stitching
Keep your needle in the spiral part of your work and lift the presser foot **(1)**. Carefully spin the spiral toward you, so your line of stitching will go at a 90-degree angle. Drop the presser foot, then stitch in a straight line through the center of the spiral, all the way to the other side.

Stitch over the line a few times to create a solid line of block stitching that will be very strong and support the bag.

Now do exactly the same thing on the other side of the spiral, so that you make an X design **(2)**. You may notice that once you've done both lines, the spiral starts to curve up slightly **(3)**. This is normal and is a sign that the stitching will support the completed bag.

The final step of the structural stitching is to enclose the X that you have made with an O **(4–5)**. So, on the last round that you stitched before creating the lines, go back over it to create the block stitching. The base of your bag is now complete.

> **TIP:** Use a ruler and a tailor's pencil to draw a straight line to follow.

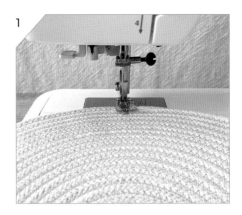

1

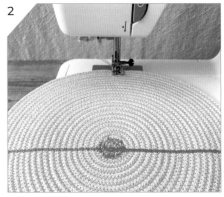

2

3

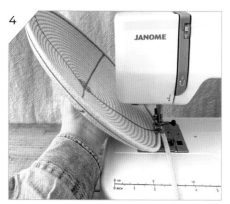

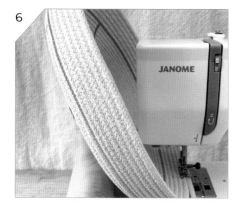

Building Shape

Support the spiral with your left hand and angle it halfway between the base and side of your machine (6). You are aiming to create an angle that will steadily encourage the bag to go gently outward and upward with each round.

Keep stitching at the same angle for approximately thirteen rounds (7). Then, on the last round, create another layer of block stitching. Now switch to the neutral thread (8).

Continue stitching and look to build the shape—aim to maintain the width you have created without going out wider. You can check the angle without taking your work off the machine, by eyeballing from the base where your left hand is supporting, all the way along to the top of the spiral.

9

10

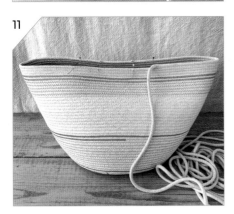

11

Since this is a larger shape, it's easy to go off your angle—but if you do, it's also easy to gently ease it back to where you want it to be, if you catch it quickly. Continue stitching in your neutral thread for about thirteen rounds.

Switch back to the bright thread and continue stitching in exactly the same way **(9)**. You are aiming to build height, since this will become the depth of your bag **(10)**. Once you've stitched another seven rounds or so, do another round of block stitching.

You are now on to the final section of your bag. In this part you will need to create the gap sections. These will become the home for your cotton-tape handles. Before you continue stitching, find the end of the rope and use a straight pin to mark out 16.4 ft. (5 m). Stitch in neutral thread to the pin marker.

Gap Sections for Adding the Handles

The technique for making these gaps is the same as in the previous projects. The trickiest part is making sure the gaps are positioned correctly on the spiral.

Take your work off the machine to mark out your gap sections. You will need to make four sections in total. The first section will start where you have just finished stitching— and your gap will need to be 0.4 in. (1 cm) wider than the width of your tape.

My sections needed to be 1.9 in. (4.8 cm), so from the point of my last stitch, I measured across and then put a straight pin in the point where I would need to start stitching again **(11)**. Now that the first section is measured, it's easier to make sure the sections are spaced equally **(12)**. Pinch the two sides of the bag together so the gap section is facing you and positioned between the

12

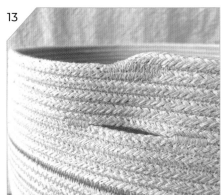

13

14

middle and right edge. Measure the distance from the right edge of the section to the end. For me, this was 5.5 in. (14 cm).

Now measure from the other side and pin-mark 5.5 in. (14 cm) from the left edge. Pin again the width of your gap section—now you have your second gap section. The two sections are equidistant to the edges of your bag. To pin-mark the other two sections, pull the sides together and use pins to mark the opposite sections in exactly the same place on the other side of the bag.

Put the bag back under the machine and stitch the rest of the first section (13). Work your way around the bag, block-stitching each gap section as you go. Be mindful that the straight pins don't scratch you as they come over the top of the machine.

Once you've stitched all the sections, continue stitching as normal until the rope runs out. If possible, try to

finish your spiral halfway through one of the gap sections. Stitch the end down firmly—it can be hidden underneath the cotton tape handles.

The stitched ropework is now complete (14)! The last job is to add the handles. The most important thing is to make sure that the two sections of cotton tape are the same length. To make long handles, use two lengths of cotton tape measuring 47 in. (120 cm) each.

Take one of the lengths and push it through the first gap—from outside to inside—and pull it up above the line of the bag (15). To make a

15

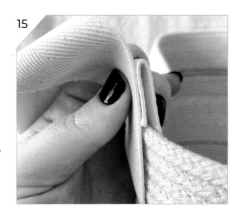

16

neat seam, fold the tape back on itself so you are pinching together three layers of cotton tape. Carefully position this under your machine and stitch down well.

Take the other end of your cotton tape length and repeat the process in the second gap. Now you have your first handle. Repeat with the other length on the opposite side.

Your bag is now complete and ready to accompany you on many summer adventures (16).

Variations and Finishes

My favorite aspect of artisan ropework is the endless possibility for experimentation and play. Now that you have worked your way through the projects, you have a strong vocabulary of techniques that you can experiment with and explore further.

In this chapter, I have outlined a few ideas for ways that you can tweak and change the designs. I strongly encourage you to play around with what you have learned so far, and see where it leads you. In this way, you will see your own creative style emerge within artisan ropework.

Throughout the book, each project had an element of shape, design, and color. These are the three areas in which you can focus your experiments in variations. Let's look at each of them in turn and think about how they can be approached slightly differently.

Shape

Shape is the main conversation in artisan ropework—creating 3-D shapes by stitching the rope to itself in a constant spiral. This is the main event.

The purpose of this book is to show the fundamentals of how to get started with artisan ropework, and the biggest part of that is learning to create different shapes. Going from the flat place mats to a large beach bag, each project has been designed to grow your confidence in artisan ropework.

Think about the objects that you have made, and examine what you would like to make next. Was there a project that you didn't quite get the hang of and want to revisit? Or did one ignite a curiosity in you, and you need to explore it further? Here are three prompts to get you started:

- Which project could you scale up to create a larger version?
- What other shapes could you try making with a 33 ft. (10 m) length of rope?
- How could you make an oval instead of a circle?

The possibilities are truly endless. Use your techniques to explore new questions and challenge yourself to make something completely different.

Design

When should you change thread color? When it runs out, or when it will look nifty in your shape? What would look best—a loop finish or a tassel finish?

Design is a process of asking a question and then finding out the answer, and the best way to do that is to experiment. Perhaps you can come up with your own unique way of finishing your work.

Loops have always been my signature because I personally love the rounded look they give, so it's a style I always come back to. Throughout the book I've given a number of different ways that you can finish your work—loops and tassels are the two main ones. Can you come up with your own special way to finish your ropework projects?

Color

I think that color is the most fun element to experiment with, because there's always a new way to look at color. Due to the vast choice of thread colors, you may well have already experimented with color during the projects. You may have your own strong preferences anyway for certain color choices and combinations.

You may have noticed that pastel colors are tricky in ropework because the rope visually drains the color away: that's why block stitching is so useful. Structurally, block stitching is an essential technique, but aesthetically it's a gift.

You may have discovered that you like color to feature throughout the shapes, or that you prefer a minimal look with only small amounts of color. In the Wall Hanging project, textile paint is used as an alternative way to create color on the rope. Thread and paint are the two most obvious choices when it comes to experimenting with color—but what about actually dyeing the rope?

Cotton rope is a natural material, and so it is possible to experiment both with natural and procion (chemical) dye. A quick internet search will give you a wealth of ideas about where to start with dye, and of course, please follow any safety advice given, especially when dyeing at home.

I have experimented with dye baths in the past, and one thing I will say is—be sure that the rope is fully dry before you stitch, and be aware that the soaking process can change the structure of the rope and make it less sturdy.

Whether you want to explore with thread colors, paint, or dye, the most important thing is to allow yourself to be swept up in the relationship between rope and color, and to see where it takes you.

Troubleshooting

I've taught a number of real-life workshops, and there are always a few common problems that come up when learning to stitch rope. Here I've shared the top ones and the easy fixes, so if you find yourself in a pickle, you can quickly get back to building those spirals.

Machine Issues

Needle snapping or bending

· Are you using a denim or heavyweight needle? If not, you should be.

· Have you remembered to lower the sewing machine's presser foot? It's easy to forget when you have the thicker rope under the machine.

· Is the needle position in the correct setting for your zigzag stitch? Check your manual for the right button or lever to press for this.

· Are you pulling too hard? It's a fine balance, and if you're pulling too hard you might be pulling the needle out of its intended trajectory, and it's snapping on the machine.

· Ideally you should change your needle after a couple of smaller projects or after every larger project. Needles can blunt or dull quickly, especially if you are sewing many meters of rope.

Thread snapping or snagging

· Are you using the right thread—a high-quality sew-all thread or a cotton one suitable for heavy fabrics? If not, you should be.

· Have you set the tension correctly? Is the thread snagging through on one side? Check if the tension setting has been knocked. This often happens when making bigger pieces, as your spiral begins to engulf the machine.

· Have you correctly threaded your machine? I know it's basic, but often the thread has just popped out somewhere, or the bobbin is in the wrong way around.

Thread isn't catching both sides of the rope

· Can you widen your zigzag stitch? Use a rope coaster or an offcut to test your stitch width and length. You need to get the balance right to catch the sides and make progress with the stitching.

· You may not be pulling the sides together tightly enough.

Machine feels heavy or is making a "thunk" noise as you sew

· Delint your machine. It's likely your needle is having trouble getting through the rope plus a big pile of lint.

· Change your needle—it might be blunt and therefore finding it hard to punch through the rope.

· Does your machine require oiling? Older domestic machines may require oiling. Zigzagging makes your machine work harder. Check your manual to see if a drop of oil is what you need to make things run smoothly again.

Shaping Issues

The spiral doesn't feel sturdy

· Check the thread tension—is it even on the topside and underside?

· Examine how you are pulling the rope. Does it feel like you are pulling the two sides together? Or does it feel a bit unruly and out of your control?

· Are you using the right type of rope? Hollow cords cannot maintain a good structure.

The spiral is becoming a barrel before the end and you can't keep sewing

· You may be pulling too tightly.

· The angle of the spiral has turned inward instead of outward. This is a problem that is experienced mostly with the larger projects, but it can occur on the last round of the smaller ones if you pull too tightly when creating that final extra tension to make your project sturdy.

Remember that artisan ropework is at all times a balance among

· the rope
· the thread
· and you

If you are experiencing an issue, the answer almost certainly will be found within one of these areas.

About the Author

Jessica has focused solely on artisan ropework since 2016. During this time she has exhibited at many events—including the prestigious Great Northern Contemporary Craft Fair. Her work has featured in a number of exhibitions at galleries throughout the UK. With numerous collections of work in her portfolio, Jessica has deeply explored the possibilities of shape and texture within this craft.

Understanding the balance among the materials, the sewing machine, and the artistry involved to create this type of work is a skill that Jessica has taken great time and care to understand. Her mastery of this balance is what gives her the capacity to be able to break it down into accessible projects that can allow anyone with basic sewing-machine skills to access this wonderful craft.

A Final Note

Now that you have reached the end of the book, I hope that *Artisan Ropework* has proved an invaluable resource for you to start on your stitched-ropework journey. For me there is nothing more exciting as an artist than a huge pile of rope and a whole day of sewing ahead of me!

When I am not elbow deep in rope and thread, you can find me online:

Website: *www.rubycubes.co.uk*
Instagram: *@rubycubes_uk*
Pinterest: *@rubycubesUK*